John Austin Stevens

The Expedition of Lafayette Against Arnold

A paper read before the Maryland Historical Society, January 14th, 1878

John Austin Stevens

The Expedition of Lafayette Against Arnold
A paper read before the Maryland Historical Society, January 14th, 1878

ISBN/EAN: 9783337322625

Printed in Europe, USA, Canada, Australia, Japan

Cover: Foto ©Andreas Hilbeck / pixelio.de

More available books at **www.hansebooks.com**

𝔉𝔲𝔫𝔡-𝔓𝔲𝔟𝔩𝔦𝔠𝔞𝔱𝔦𝔬𝔫, 𝔑𝔬. 13.

THE

Expedition of Lafayette

AGAINST ARNOLD.

A Paper read before the Maryland Historical Society

January 14th, 1878.

BY

JOHN AUSTIN STEVENS.

LIBRARIAN, NEW YORK HISTORICAL SOCIETY.

𝔅𝔞𝔩𝔱𝔦𝔪𝔬𝔯𝔢, 1878.

EXPEDITION OF LAFAYETTE

AGAINST ARNOLD.

THE standard histories of the United States contain but brief allusion to the interesting episode in the Southern campaign of 1781, which may be properly termed the expedition of Lafayette against Arnold. Although unsuccessful, it was the beginning of a series of skilful manœuvres which ended in the capture of Cornwallis, at Yorktown, and virtually secured the independence of the thirteen colonies.

The naval operations of the French fleet have been carefully detailed, but some new light is also thrown on these by M. le Capitaine Chevalier, in his recent exhaustive history of the French Marine during the war of American Independence, published at Paris, last year.

2

On the other hand the land operations of the expedition have received but brief and passing notice from our historians, Gordon, Marshall, and later, from Irving and Bancroft. The English accounts of Andrews and Stedman, supply no additional information.

In the papers and correspondence of Lieut. Colonel Ebenezer Stevens, who commanded the artillery upon this expedition, now in the keeping of the New York Historical Society, sufficient details are to be found to supply the missing links and render a complete account of the campaign possible.

Lafayette, as the leader of the expedition, is naturally the central figure about which are grouped its personages and incidents. A word concerning him and the reasons for his selection to command its movements, will give direction and point to the narrative.

Lafayette immediately on his arrival at Philadelphia, in July, 1777, placed himself at the disposal of Congress upon two conditions, viz: of serving without pay and as a volunteer. Notwithstanding the prejudice entertained by the Americans against the pretensions of the French officers who were already in service, and disregarding the extreme youth of the young nobleman who had just completed his twentieth year, Congress touched by the generosity of the proposal and impressed by the importance of the acquisition of a name so illustrious in its history and connections, by a resolution of the 31st July, 1777, in which they expressly state these reasons for their action, gave him the rank and commission of Major General in the army of the United States.

Presented to Washington at a Congressional dinner, he was at once distinguished by him, attached to head-quarters and made a part of the military family of the Commander-in-Chief. Following Washington through the whole of the campaign of this year, he was wounded in the leg at the battle of the Brandywine, and narrowly escaped capture in the disorderly rout of the American troops.

Recovered from his wound, the young soldier joined General Greene, who was manœuvring to hold Cornwallis in check in the Jerseys. There he distinguished himself in a sharp action, the result of a reconnoissance in force, in which he surprised and routed a corps of Hessians at Gloucester Point.

This brilliant little affair increased his popularity with the army and the country, and on the 1st December following, the Congress passed a resolution informing General Washington that it was highly agreeable to them that the Marquis de Lafayette, be appointed to the command of a division in the Continental army.

The winter of 1777–1778, was passed at Valley
Forge. In January, the Congress resolved to
follow up the victory at Saratoga, and to use its
own words to make "an irruption into Canada."
From the very outset of hostilities, the colonists
had been alive to the immediate and prospective
dangers of a hostile occupation of the long exposed
frontier line, with every inch of which the ances-
tral struggle with New France had made them
familiar. Desirous to recompense the gallant
young officer for his disinterested zeal, which he
was daily showing in the exposure of his person
and the free use of his ample fortune, Congress,
on the 23d January, the day following their original resolution, elected him to conduct the expedition into Canada with Major General Conway and
General Stark, as his aids.

In a letter to his wife of the 3rd February,
Lafayette expressed the joy he felt at his appointment to the independent command of three
thousand men, with the title of General of the
Northern army, and at the thought that he was
about to march to the deliverance of New France
from the yoke which oppressed her. His illusions
of conquest were soon dissipated. No laurels, he
wrote to Washington, seemed likely to sprout on
Lake Champlain in the severe season. Arrived at
Albany, the head-quarters of the Northern army,
he found nothing ready except the artillery, and

in the condition of the department no hope of getting enough men in line for a *coup de main*, while Carleton, the sagacious Governor of Canada, was strengthening himself to meet any organized movement. Yielding to the reasonings of Schuyler, Lincoln and Arnold, he wrote to Congress, who had already become alarmed at the possible consequences of an ill-advised movement, abandoning the expedition, and to Washington complaining of the disagreeable and ridiculous situation in which he found himself.

For his prompt and unselfish conduct, he received the thanks of Congress and of the Board of War.

The approach of spring bringing with it preparations for a new campaign, Lafayette was by secret resolution of Congress recalled to the southward, where on the 2d May, he had the satisfaction, clad in a white scarf and accompanied by all the French officers, of announcing to the army at head-quarters, the acknowledgment of the Independence of the United States, by France, and the conclusion of a treaty of alliance with that power. During the summer, he displayed considerable military ability in the conduct of some minor movements, was conspicuous for his bravery at Monmouth, and later received the thanks of Congress for his services and zeal in the expedition against Rhode Island.

Although he was at this time the third general officer in Washington's army, the young commander seems to have desired a larger field and more independence of action. When wounded, he spent the hours of his confinement in digesting a plan which he proposed to the French ministry for the conquest of the Indies. Now, that the recognition of American Independence, by France, had led to hostilities between that power and Great Britain, he felt that his services were due to his native country, asked and received an unlimited leave of absence. The king placed the Alliance of thirty-six guns at his disposition for his return.

On his departure, Congress recommended him to His Majesty, by special letter, signed by its President, as "wise in council, brave in the field, and patient in the fatigue of war." In addition, no doubt at his own instance, the French ministry was urged to undertake an expedition against Canada with French troops under the command of Lafayette, and coöperation was promised from the American lines.

Arrived in France, February, 1779, the Marquis was received with every mark of distinction. The French ministry would not hear, however, to an expedition against Canada. They already dreaded the too great aggrandizement of the United States. Finding his arguments and appeals of no avail,

the impetuous and persistent Marquis demanded
and obtained an expeditionary corps of four thousand men, who were intrusted to the charge of
the Count de Rochambeau, and embarked on
board a fleet of seven vessels, under command of
Admiral de Ternay, early in 1780. Lafayette
preceded their arrival in America, by a few days.
We now find the French alliance a factor in
American Independence, owing to the persist-
ence of Lafayette; and his own scruples as to
foreign service while his own country was at war,
happily dissolved.

During the campaign of 1780, the American
army was divided into three corps, one guarding
the defences of the Hudson and the post of West
Point, under the command of Arnold; another in
the Carolinas, first under Gates, and later under
Greene, and a third in the Jerseys, under the
immediate order of Washington. To this Lafayette was again attached in command of the
light infantry which composed the advance guard
of the army.

An account of the origin and formation of this
famous corps, naturally finds a place in this
narrative.

In the summer of 1777, when the Northern
army was being recruited to resist the advance
of Burgoyne, Washington seeing the necessity of
a light corps to check the savages in the British

employ who hung upon the flanks of the American
army, dispatched to Gates, then in command at
Stillwater, Colonel Morgan with his rifle corps.
This body was made up of frontiersmen accus-
tomed to the use of weapons at long range and
the Indian mode of warfare. They had been
chosen from the entire army. To this corps,
Gates added two hundred and fifty bayonets,
carefully picked, and placed them under Major
Dearborn. This *corps d'élite* did noteworthy service in the several actions which culminated in
the victory of Saratoga; service so eminent that
the importance of nourishing and strengthening
it, was at once recognized.

Placed under the command of Lafayette, it
was increased by the same process of judicious
selection to two thousand men. The Marquis
de Chastellux, who visited Lafayette's camp on
the Totowa, in November of this year, (1780,)
gives an interesting account of this picked command.

"This troop," he says, "made a good appearance, and were better clothed than the rest of
the army; the uniforms, both of the officers and
soldiers, smart and military, each soldier wearing
a helmet of hard leather with a crest of horse
hair. The officers armed with espontoons, or
rather half pikes, and the subalterns with fusils,
but both are provided with short and light sabres

brought from France, and made a present to them
by Marquis de Lafayette." The plumes, we find
elsewhere, were black and red. The flags were
also brought from France; one bore a cannon
with the device *Ultima Ratio;* another, a laurel
crown and civic crown, blended with the device,
No Other; others bore emblems of a similar general character.

Heath, in his memoir, credits the corps of light
infantry "as being perhaps as fine a body of men
as ever was formed." "Major General, the Marquis de Lafayette," he adds, "had with infinite
pains and great expense, endeavored to render
them respectable in their appearance as well as
discipline in which he was nobly seconded by
the officers." Lafayette was the idol of the
corps. Before he left America for France, to
secure the assistance which had now so endeared
him to the army and the country, he had already
earned the title of "the soldier's friend." The
operation of the campaign, however, did not afford
of any opportunity for distinction.

On the 23rd November, the main body of the
army separated to move into winter quarters; the
light infantry corps was broken up for the winter,
and the men ordered to join.their respective regiments.

Early in December, General Washington took
winter head-quarters at New Windsor, a few miles

3

to the northward of West Point, where, on the 12th, information reached him that an expedition was about to sail from New York under the command of Generals Arnold and Phillips.

One of the conditions of the bargain between the traitor Arnold and Sir Henry Clinton, for the surrender of the post of West Point, was a commission of Colonel of a regiment with the rank of Brigadier General in the British army. Arriving at New York after his narrow escape, he at once endeavored to display his new born zeal and *loyalty*, if such rank treason to friends and country deserve the name.

Beginning with an address to the inhabitants of America, in explanation of the reasons for his desertion from their cause, which he published in the tory sheets of Rivington, Gaine and Robertson, on the 7th October. He next issued on the 20th, a proclamation inviting enlistments into a corps of calvary and infantry, to be commanded by himself, and offered a bounty of three guineas to each non-commissioned officer and private.

On the 21st December, Sir Henry Clinton dispatched Arnold with a fleet of fifty sail, having on board a force of sixteen hundred men to replace the command of General Leslie who had gone to the aid of Cornwallis in the Carolinas.

Arriving in the James river on the 2d of January, Arnold landed fifteen hundred men, and

a few light horse, fifteen miles below Richmond,
and marched into that town at twelve o'clock
on the morning of the 5th of January, and de-
destroyed the public buildings and stores.
Falling back immediately, he continued the
ravage of the country from the fleet. Landing
again on the 15th, he marched to Smithfield, and
thence proceeded to Portsmouth where he took
post on the 25th, and began to fortify.
Congress perceiving the danger of permitting
the enemy to gain a permanent footing in the
important colony of Virginia, and aware of the
deficiency of military stores, had on the 1st
January, passed a resolution which was communicated on the 2d, to Washington, directing a
movement of part of his troops, including the
allied forces, under Rochambeau, to counteract
the views of the enemy.
The mutiny of the Pennsylvania line, however,
prevented any immediate action, and the blockade
of the French squadron at Newport by a superior
force rendered it highly improbable that the commanders would be willing to divide their forces.
A march by land seemed, therefore, to be the
only practicable mode of coöperation to which
the season, length of way, badness of roads and
difficulty of transportation, offered weighty objections.

Meanwhile, a fortuitous circumstance changed the condition of affairs. While cruising in pursuit of the French frigates on their way from Boston, to reinforce the squadron at Newport, two of the four British vessels met with disaster. The- Culloden, a seventy-four gun ship, was wrecked upon the coast of Long Island, in a violent storm. The Bedford, also a seventy-four, dismasted, and the America driven to sea and for a long time not heard of. This mishap, and the arrival of the frigates from Boston equalizing the rival forces, Monsieur Destouches, on whom the command of the fleet had devolved upon the death of Admiral de Ternay, the December previous, resolved to take advantage of the opportunity.

Having first ascertained that the British fleet was still too strong for a direct attack to be risked upon it, he resolved to execute the scheme proposed to him, by the Chevalier de la Luzerne, at the request of the Governor of Virginia and Congress, to relieve Virginia. Rochambeau offered to send a division of land forces, but the necessity of military coöperation at this time did not appear, the militia being supposed sufficient to protect the country.

He dispatched M. de Tilly, with his ship L'Eveille, of seventy-four guns, accompanied by the frigates Gentille, Surveillante and the cutter

La Guèpe, to the Chesapeake, with orders to destroy the flotilla with the aid of which Arnold was ravaging the coasts of Virginia. M. de Tilly failed in his mission, the flotilla escaping beyond his reach up the Elizabeth river.

He therefore at once set sail on his return, which was all the more necessary since Admiral Arburthnot having repaired his vessels, had reappeared at the station on Gardiner's bay. On his return to Newport harbor, M. de Tilly fell in with and captured the Romulus, of fifty-four guns, a sloop and some transports which he took safely to port, where he arrived at the close of the month.

Early in February, advices from Count Rochambeau to Washington, encouraged him to believe that Monsieur Destouches was inclined to a combined movement to the southward. Postponing his intended departure for Newport, he at once set about organizing an expedition. On the 14th, the Count de la Maime arrived at head-quarters with letters from Rochambeau, to which Washington replied the day following, giving his views as to the proper mode of conducting a campaign and advising him that he had put under marching orders a detachment of twelve hundred men who should advance in a few days towards the head of Elk river, there to embark and proceed to a coöperation. He expressed the opinion that it would reach the destined place of operation in about four weeks from the date of his letter. The same day he directed General Heath to have all the light companies under his command completed to fifty rank and file each, and to assemble the whole without delay at Peekskill; ready with shoes and other necessaries for a march to Morristown. He directed that the men should be robust, suited for expeditious movement, and in other respects well chosen; the officers to carry light baggage only.

On the 17th, the light companies were formed into battalions in the following order: the eight oldest companies of the Massachusetts line to form a battalion under the command of Colonel Vose and Major Galvan; the two youngest companies of that line with those of Connecticut and Rhode Island, to form a battalion under the command of Colonel Gamat and Major Thorp; those of the New Hampshire line and Colonel Hazen's regiment, and such others as might be joined to them to form a battalion. This appointment of officers was declared to be intended not to affect the general plan of arranging the light infantry for the campaign.

On the 18th, Washington advised De Rochambeau, that the destruction of Arnold's corps was of such immense importance to the welfare of the Southern states that he had resolved to attempt

it, with the detachment ordered thither in conjunction with the militia, even without the aid of the French troops, *provided* M. Destouches could protect the operation by commanding Chesapeake bay, and preventing reinforcement of the enemy from New York.

On the 18th, the light companies were inspected. On the 20th, a detachment of artillery was ordered from the post at New Windsor, to join the detachment of light infantry, and the command given to the Marquis de Lafayette, who, chafing at inactivity and eager for distinction, had been long anxious to engage at the southward, but had yielded to the desire of Washington, that he should remain at head-quarters were his influence with the French officers was of paramount importance. While this detachment was preparing at Peekskill, a second was formed at Morristown from the Jersey troops. The two amounted to twelve hundred, rank and file.

Washington gave his final instruction to Lafayette, on the 20th. He was directed to march by battalions and rendezvous at Pompton. From Trenton, the water route by the Delaware to Christiana Bridge, Marcus Hook or Chester was recommended if the river was not open. The route to be arranged in concert with the Quartermaster General. No delay to be suffered because of the want of provisions; all necessaries to be

obtained by military impress, if necessary; vessels to be ready on his arrival at the head of Elk to convey him down the bay to Hampton Roads, or to the point of operations, and a previous communication to be opened with the French fleet which Monsieur Destouches had despatched on the 9th. No terms to be made with Arnold, but summary execution to be done upon him should he fall into the hands of the Marquis.

The command of the artillery destined for the expedition was assigned to Lieutenant Colonel Ebenezer Stevens, of the second battalion of artillery, an officer distinguished for merit and rare energy from the beginning of the war. The Marquis de Lafayette had especially requested that he should accompany him in this capacity. On the 19th, Colonel Stevens was directed by General Knox, chief of artillery, to repair to Philadelphia, and there apply to the Board of War for cannon, ordnance and military stores, and to have them ready for transport in five or or six days. The requisition included four field pieces six pounders, four eighteen pounders, three twenty-four pounders, one eight, and two or three five inch howitzers, besides small arms, ammunition and military stores. He further advises the detachment from the post at New Windsor of one captain, one captain's lieutenant, three subalterns, and sixty non-commissioned officers and matrosses.

General Knox adds that the Marquis had engaged
to make good the deficiency of artillery men from
his command.

On the 20th, Knox informed Stevens that the
Commander-in-Chief had consented to allow the
two eight inch mortars to be taken from the
artillery park for the expedition, and that they
would be conveyed to him in a covered wagon.
The detachment set off without delay. Washington informed the Chevalier Destouches, on
the 22d, that they had marched, and that they
would arrive at the head of Elk by the 5th or
6th of March. This the Marquis reminded Washington in a letter from Philadelphia, of the 24th,
was the shortest calculation, at the same time
advising him that notwithstanding the extreme
badness of the roads, the march had been performed with such order and alacrity that two
men only had been left behind, and even these
two had been later embarked with the baggage.
The detachment was at Pompton on the 23d.
The march from Morristown to Princeton was
made in two days. The men embarked at Trenton on the 1st, passed Philadelphia on the 2d, and
reached the head of the Elk with the artillery
consisting of twelve heavy pieces, four six pounders and two small howitzers, on the 3d, having
made the march from Morristown in five days;
at every halt they found food and cover ready

4

prepared by the patriotic and willing inhabitants. At Philadelphia, Lafayette learned of the uncertainty of M. de Tilly's movement with his vessels, and already expressed some doubt of the success of the undertaking "My expectations," he writes Washington, "are not great, and I think we have but few chances for us." He promised to make "all possible despatch and listen particularly to the voice of prudence." "However," he adds, "some risk must be run."

To make success more sure, Washington, on the 22d February, instructed General St. Clair to raise a battalion of eight companies of fifty, rank and file, each, and forward them to the Marquis with despatch. This was in accordance also with the resolve of Congress, that the Pennsylvania line should make part of the southern army.

On the 27th February, a despatch from Count de Rochambeau, reached Washington, at New Windsor, informing him of the return of the vessels under de Tilly, from the Chesapeake to Newport. Without the delay of a moment, Washington communicated this intelligence to Lafayette with an additional caution of which the sequel will show the necessity. In it will be found a remarkable instance of the sagacity amounting to prevision, foreknowledge even, which was the distinguishing characteristic of the large, even balanced mind of the great chief.

"Upon your arrival at the head of Elk," he writes the Marquis, "you will immediately embark the troops if the transports are ready, that not a moment's time be lost after you receive certain advices that our friends are below. *But until that matter is ascertained beyond a doubt you will on no account leave Elk river.*

The French squadron was expected to sail again without delay.

On his arrival at the head of Elk, Lafayette received every offer of assistance from the State of Maryland and the patriotic Governor Thomas Sim Lee, and the deficiencies in the quartermaster's and engineer's departments were amply supplied. A little fleet was gradually gathered together, all but three bay craft, and, of these three, the largest, the Admiral's ship mounted only twelve guns. To relieve himself of the naval command, the Marquis sent for Commodore Nicholson, of Baltimore.

On the evening of the 7th March, a despatch from Washington of the 1st, announced to Lafayette the intention of De Rochambeau and the Chevalier Destouches, to operate in the Chesapeake with their whole fleet and a detachment of eleven hundred French troops, grenadiers and chasseurs included. The Chevalier was expected to sail on the 5th.

Washington informed Lafayette, however, that the Chevalier had made some difficulty about sending a frigate up the bay to convey his flotilla to the scene of operations; notwithstanding this, the certainty of the coöperation of the French fleet, determined the Marquis to transport his detachment to Annapolis.

Commodore Nicholson cheerfully responded to the request of the Marquis, and hastened to Annapolis to make disposition for the movement of the detachment.

Constant winds, heavy rains, disappointments of vessels and inconveniences of every kind continued to delay the embarkation until the 9th, when protected by the Nesbitt of twelve guns, the cannon on board the vessels which carried Colonel Stevens, and two vessels which came to meet them from Baltimore, armed respectively with six and eight guns, the little fleet set sail piloted by Captain Martin, of the Nesbitt. The transports dropped down the river and crossing the Chesapeake arrived safely in the harbor of Annapolis, the Capital of the State of Maryland, the following evening.

The Marquis himself embarked on the Dauphin, a little vessel armed with swivels and manned by thirty soldiers.

Preceding the fleet to Annapolis where he was met by intelligence, he sailed down the Chesa-

peake to concert a plan with the French fleet
and secure the despatch of a frigate up the bay
to convoy his troops. He was well aware of the
personal risk he incurred, but felt the matter to
be of such importance that he not only waived
all such considerations, but took with him the
only son of the minister of the French marine
to give weight to his negotiations with the fleet
commanders.

Landing at Williamsburg, he found to his sur-
prise that no fleet had made its appearance.
While waiting its appearance he set to work to
raise a military force of five thousand men with
whose aid the capture of Portsmouth and Arnold
seemed a certainty.

While the gallant young Frenchman was dis-
playing his customary zeal, activity, and prudence
in the execution of his mission, Washington, who
was more than usually solicitous for his success,
which as he wrote to him, "he most ardently
wished not only on the public, but his own
account," neglected nothing which could con-
tribute to it.

On the 2d March, the day after receiving letters
from the French commanders proposing a general
movement southward, Washington set out from
New Windsor for Rhode Island. He arrived at
Newport on the morning of the 6th, taking with
him intelligence of the completion of the con-

federation of the thirteen states in Congress, on the 1st instant. Everything combined to make his reception brilliant in the gay and fashionable capital. At the ferry at Jamestown, he was received by the Admiral's barge and conducted on board his ship where he was met by General Rochambeau, the Admiral and the French officer. Salutes of cannon were fired from the ships, and upon his landing at Long-wharf by the north battery. Passing through the lines of the garrison, all of the troops of which were drawn up, he was escorted to the head-quarters of General Rochambeau, where in consequence of direct orders from the Court of Versailles, he received all the honors ever paid to the Prince Royal or a Marshal of France; greater than which can only be tendered to the king. In the evening, the town and the fleet in the harbor were beautifully illuminated, and the highest pleasure and satisfaction appeared in every countenance. Such is the account in well ordered old time phrase which appeared in the newspapers of the day.

Washington reached Newport in the forenoon, and before he landed at one o'clock, from the ship of Monsieur Destouches, it was agreed that a detachment should at once be placed on board the men of war by De Rochambeau, and the command entrusted to the Baron de Vioménil.

The next day the wind was favorable as possible to the French, and as adverse to the English as it could blow, but a want of supplies did not permit advantage to be taken of it, and it was not until the evening of the 8th, that Destouches set sail with one line of battle ship eighty guns, two seventy-fours, four sixty-fours, one thirty-two, and the Romulus, of forty-four guns, the late prize of Captain de Tilly, which had been repaired and armed, (in all 560 guns.)

Meanwhile, Sir Henry Clinton at New York, had learned with alarm of the progress southward of the detachment under Lafayette, and had immediately given notice to Vice-Admiral Arburthnot, who commanded the fleet at Gardiner's bay, submitting to him the propriety of detaching a proper number of ships to clear the Chesapeake, if he had not already done so.

Arburthnot was aware on the 8th of the French movement and their point of destination, and on the 9th, the squadron dropped down to the entrance of the bay; weighing anchor on the morning of the 10th, and hoisting his pennant on board the London, he followed in pursuit with one line of battle ship of ninety-eight guns, three of seventy-four, three of sixty-four, one of fifty; in all, eight ships carrying 562 guns. Frigates accompanied each fleet to serve as signal vessels.

It has been said that the weight of metal was in favor of the British, and the number of men was larger on board the French fleet, but the official reports do not bear out this statement. On the contrary, the two squadrons appear to have been fairly matched.

The rival fleets made all speed with a southward breeze, the English to windward of the French. The wind changing to the northwest, the English hauled close to and rapidly gained upon the French vessels which they overtook early on the morning of the 16th, about sixty miles distant from the Capes of the Chesapeake. The weather had been foggy, and the French commander felt himself close to the harbor, when the fog lifting, the enemy was seen close upon the rear. The sea ran high, and the French manœuvred to obtain the weather guage, so that it was not until half past two o'clock that the fleets came within gunshot of each other, when the Chevalier Destouches, a sailor of first order, who had greatly distinguished himself at the combat of Ouessant, gave signal for action. A sharp contest ensued, in which the van of the British line was severely handled, when Arburthnot shortening sail to cover his crippled ships, and the fog again settling, the squadrons separated, both holding their course towards the land, and neither showing any disposition to renew the engagement. During the night Admiral Arburthnot entered the Chesapeake, and anchored his squadron in Lynn Haven bay. The next morning the French officers met in council, and concluded that in consequence of the severe damage sustained by the Conquérant and the Ardent, a return to Newport was imperatively necessary. The honors were with the French squadron who held the scene of action, but the advantage all to the English who succeeded in blocking the Chesapeake, and preventing the success of the combined operations.

In reviewing this naval contest, Monsieur Chevalier correctly ascribes the unfortunate result of the affair to the failure of the French Marine to apply to their vessels the improvements adopted by the English. The higher sailing qualities of the latter being clearly manifested in the chase and the action.

This affair was differently received in different countries. Captain Destouches, who by all precedent was entitled to promotion to Chef d'Escadre, received a pension but no increase of rank, nor was any accorded to his officers. This sufficiently marked the dissatisfaction of the French Court. On the other hand, the English Admiralty, who could not endure the thought that a British squadron had gained no advantage in an action with the French on equal terms, severely

5

censured Admiral Arburthnot, and ordered him
home. For their part, the American Congress,
notwithstanding their disappointment, expressed
their satisfaction on the 5th April, by a resolution directing that the President transmit the
thanks of the United States in Congress assem-
bled, to the Count de Rochambeau and the Chevalier Destouches, commanders of the army and
fleet sent by his Most Christian Majesty to the
succor of his allies, for the zeal and vigilance
they have on every occasion manifested to fulfil
the generous instructions of their Sovereign and
the expectations of the United States; that he
present their particular thanks to the Chevalier
Destouches, and the officers and men under his
command for the bravery, firmness, and good
conduct displayed in the late enterprise against
the enemy at Portsmouth, in Virginia; in which,
although the accomplishment of the object was
prevented by unforeseen events, the arduous contest so gallantly and advantageously maintained
on the 16th March last, off the Capes of Chesapeake bay, against a superior British fleet, does
honor to the arms of his Most Christian Majesty,
and is a happy presage of decisive advantage to
the United States.

Lafayette having made his preliminary dispo-
sitions, visited the camp of General Muhlenburg,
near Suffolk, and found that Arnold had taken

position near Portsmouth. Advancing his troops to examine the enemy's works a slight skirmish took place. Lafayette had resolved to make a more complete reconnoisance on the 21st, but was surprised by information from Major McPherson, that a fleet had just come to anchor within the capes. He was in hopes that it was the French fleet as Arnold seemed in great alarm, and long hesitated to approach the vessels notwithstanding their signals. Soon however, all doubt was dispelled, and the Marquis realized the unwelcome truth that the object of the expedition was frustrated. The militia was immediately withdrawn to their original positions; Baron Steuben, with whose command Lafayette had been prudent not to interfere, was requested to take measures for the safety of the military stores which had been accumulated, and Lafayette sent up orders to Annapolis to the detachment of light infantry, too valuable a body of men to be lightly risked, being the *élite* of the army, to be ready to move at a moment's notice.

Washington's foresight and Lafayette's error of judgment now became apparent. On the 5th, Washington expressed his regret that Lafayette "had gone out of the Elk," while with his usual generosity, he acknowledged "that the move to Annapolis, was certainly judicious." In this letter he recalled the detachment. When Lafayette

came to execute this order and move his command, he found insuperable obstacles; there were
no boats to cross over the ferries, no wagons or
horses to be had, and the passage of the bay by
the way they had come prevented by the two
British sloops of war, the "Hope," of twenty
guns, and the "Monk," of eighteen guns, which
Arburthnot had detached from his squadron, immediately on his arrival, to scour the bay and
blockade the harbor.

The papers of Colonel Stevens supply a graphic
picture of the difficulties of the situation. His
account is to be found in a letter addressed to
Jeremiah Wadsworth and Jonathan Trumbull, a
committee of Congress, in 1790, and again in a
letter to Benj. Staddert, Secretary of the Navy,
in 1798, in reply to a request for his opinion of
gunboats as naval defences.

From these it appears that the little American
fleet consisted of ninety-seven sail of river craft,
all blockaded by the two vessels of the enemy.
Repeated councils of war were held, and retreat
by water was pronounced impracticable. Return
by land seemed the only feasible manner, but how
to remove the heavy artillery and stores? Officers
were sent into the interior to procure teams for
the purpose, but after remaining out ten days,
they returned without having been able to procure any. Even had they been procured the

movement of the heavy artillery over country roads broken by spring rains would have been almost impossible. Washington, himself well acquainted with the nature of the country, expressed his anxiety on this score.

Finally, at another council, Colonel Stevens submitted a plan to drive the British blockading vessels from the harbor, and thus open the way for a water passage to the head of Elk. Objections were at first made for fear that the vessels used might be lost and needless expense incurred, but Governor Lee, with whom Colonel Stevens had contracted a warm personal friendship during his stay, offering to pay for them should they be lost or injured, the Marquis authorized the Colonel to put his project in execution. Taking two sloops of about sixty-two tons burthen, Colonel Stevens fitted them with two eighteen pounders each in their bows, and a travelling forge in their holds, and raised an awning upon their decks to protect the men against fire from the enemy's rigging. So expeditiously was this performed that at the end of three days all was ready. At ten o'clock on the morning of the 6th of April, the vessels were manned by two hundred volunteers each, and set out under the charge of Commodore Nicholson. On their approach, the British vessels not apparently relishing the hot shot of the Americans, left their moorings and dropping down the bay opened the passage for the detachment which embarked on the fleet and protected by the improvised gunboats, reached the head of Elk the same night. There is little doubt but for this brilliant manœuvre, the fleet and artillery would, on the withdrawal of the troops, have fallen into hands of the enemy, and the defenceless city of Annapolis have been plundered and burned. Such at the time was the opinion of Governor Lee.

Arrived at the head of Elk, Lafayette found letters from Washington, countermanding the order of recall and ordering him southward to the aid of General Greene, who was being hard pressed by Cornwallis, in the Carolinas. This change of plan was agreed upon at a general council of war, it being apparent that the summer campaign would hinge on the southern movements. Lafayette was now in a very difficult situation; his troops all drawn from northern regiments, were extremely discontented at the order to join the southern army; they were ill-clad; without shoes, and were waiting for their pay from the States. They had cheerfully engaged upon a short expedition and now found themselves at the opening of a summer campaign in a hot climate and unhealthy country. Under these dispiriting circumstances, Lafayette showed his really remarkable qualities. When he left Susquehanna Ferry, it was the general opinion that he would not reach Baltimore with more than six hundred men. An order of the day appealing to the affection of his troops and holding up to scorn the crime of desertion was issued, and an example made by the hanging of one deserter, while two other minor delinquents were reprimanded and pardoned. In this manner, by a happy blending of authority and amenity, he regained the obedience and the confidence of his troops.

Here the monograph which has been attempted properly ends, but not in this patriotic city nor before this audience, can the next scene in the moving drama be omitted.

On the arrival of the Marquis at Baltimore, the merchants cheerfully and promptly advanced him the sum of two thousand guineas on his own responsibility. At a ball, given in his honor, he made a personal appeal to the ladies to supply garments for his men. They at once responded in a manner as practical as it was generous and cordial.

"The next day," says Scharf, in his Chronicles of Baltimore, "the ball room, which in the evening had been the scene of revelry and gaiety, was turned into a clothing manufactory." Materials were purchased with the sum advanced to the Marquis, and shirts, frocks and overalls, were cut and fashioned by the fair hands of the ladies of the city.

The recollection of this patriotic and generous movement was never effaced from the heart of the gallant Marquis. Of this he gave evidence when on his second visit to the United States as a guest of the nation, he again enjoyed the hospitality of this charming city. At an entertainment given in his honor, the Marquis proposed this graceful sentiment:

"*The Baltimore Ladies:* the old gratitude of a young soldier mingles with the respectful sense of the obligations conferred on a veteran."